Scott

Science

The Diamond Edition

PEARSON
Scott
Foresman

Editorial Offices: Glenview, Illinois • Parsippany, New Jersey • New York, New York
Sales Offices: Boston, Massachusetts • Duluth, Georgia • Glenview, Illinois
Coppell, Texas • Sacramento, California • Mesa, Arizona
www.pearsonsuccessnet.com

Series Authors

Dr. Timothy Cooney
Professor of Earth Science and Science Education
University of Northern Iowa (UNI)
Cedar Falls, Iowa

Dr. Jim Cummins
Professor
Department of Curriculum, Teaching, and Learning
University of Toronto
Toronto, Canada

Dr. James Flood
Distinguished Professor of Literacy and Language
School of Teacher Education
San Diego State University
San Diego, California

Barbara Kay Foots, M.Ed.
Science Education Consultant
Houston, Texas

Dr. M. Jenice Goldston
Associate Professor of Science Education
Department of Elementary Education Programs
University of Alabama
Tuscaloosa, Alabama

Dr. Shirley Gholston Key
Associate Professor of Science Education
Instruction and Curriculum Leadership Department
College of Education
University of Memphis
Memphis, Tennessee

Dr. Diane Lapp
Distinguished Professor of Reading and Language Arts in Teacher Education
San Diego State University
San Diego, California

Sheryl A. Mercier
Classroom Teacher
Dunlap Elementary School
Dunlap, California

Karen L. Ostlund, Ph.D.
UTeach Specialist
College of Natural Sciences
The University of Texas at Austin
Austin, Texas

Dr. Nancy Romance
Professor of Science Education & Principal Investigator
NSF/IERI Science IDEAS Project
Charles E. Schmidt College of Science
Florida Atlantic University
Boca Raton, Florida

Dr. William Tate
Chair and Professor of Education and Applied Statistics
Department of Education
Washington University
St. Louis, Missouri

Dr. Kathryn C. Thornton
Former NASA Astronaut Professor
School of Engineering and Applied Science
University of Virginia
Charlottesville, Virginia

Dr. Leon Ukens
Professor Emeritus
Department of Physics, Astronomy, and Geosciences
Towson University
Towson, Maryland

Steve Weinberg
Consultant
Connecticut Center for Advanced Technology
East Hartford, Connecticut

ISBN–13: 978-0-328-28957-8 (SVE), ISBN–10: 0-328-28957-4 (SVE);
ISBN–13: 978-0-328-30430-1 (A), ISBN–10: 0-328-30430-1 (A);
ISBN–13: 978-0-328-30431-8 (B), ISBN–10: 0-328-30431-X (B);
ISBN–13: 978-0-328-30432-5 (C), ISBN–10: 0-328-30432-8 (C);
ISBN–13: 978-0-328-30433-2 (D), ISBN–10: 0-328-30433-6 (D)

Consulting Author

Dr. Michael P. Klentschy
Superintendent
El Centro Elementary School District
El Centro, California

Science Content Consultants

Dr. Frederick W. Taylor
Senior Research Scientist
Institute for Geophysics
Jackson School of Geosciences
The University of Texas at Austin
Austin, Texas

Dr. Ruth E. Buskirk
Senior Lecturer
School of Biological Sciences
The University of Texas at Austin
Austin, Texas

Dr. Cliff Frohlich
Senior Research Scientist
Institute for Geophysics
Jackson School of Geosciences
The University of Texas at Austin
Austin, Texas

Brad Armosky
McDonald Observatory
The University of Texas at Austin
Austin, Texas

NASA Content Consultants

Adena Williams Loston, Ph.D.
Chief Education Officer
Office of the Chief Education Officer

Clifford W. Houston, Ph.D.
Deputy Chief Education Officer for Education Programs
Office of the Chief Education Officer

Frank C. Owens
Senior Policy Advisor
Office of the Chief Education Officer

Deborah Brown Biggs
Manager, Education Flight Projects Office
Space Operations Mission Directorate, Education Lead

Erika G. Vick
NASA Liaison to Pearson Scott Foresman
Education Flight Projects Office

William E. Anderson
Partnership Manager for Education
Aeronautics Research Mission Directorate

Anita Krishnamurthi
Program Planning Specialist
Space Science Education and Outreach Program

Bonnie J. McClain
Chief of Education
Exploration Systems Mission Directorate

Diane Clayton, Ph.D.
Program Scientist
Earth Science Education

Deborah Rivera
Strategic Alliances Manager
Office of Public Affairs
NASA Headquarters

Douglas D. Peterson
Public Affairs Officer, Astronaut Office
Office of Public Affairs
NASA Johnson Space Center

Nicole Cloutier
Public Affairs Officer, Astronaut Office
Office of Public Affairs
NASA Johnson Space Center

Dr. Jennifer J. Wiseman
Hubble Space Telescope Program Scientist
NASA Headquarters

Reviewers

Dr. Maria Aida Alanis
Administrator
Austin ISD
Austin Texas

Melissa Barba
Teacher
Wesley Mathews Elementary
Miami, Florida

Dr. Marcelline Barron
Supervisor/K-12 Math
and Science
Fairfield Public Schools
Fairfield, Connecticut

Jane Bates
Teacher
Hickory Flat Elementary
Canton, Georgia

Denise Bizjack
Teacher
Dr. N. H. Jones Elementary
Ocala, Florida

Latanya D. Bragg
Teacher
Davis Magnet School
Jackson, Mississippi

Richard Burton
Teacher
George Buck Elementary
School 94
Indianapolis, Indiana

Dawn Cabrera
Teacher
E.W.F. Stirrup School
Miami, Florida

Barbara Calabro
Teacher
Compass Rose Foundation
Ft. Myers, Florida

Lucille Calvin
Teacher
Weddington Math &
Science School
Greenville, Mississippi

Patricia Carmichael
Teacher
Teasley Middle School
Canton, Georgia

Martha Cohn
Teacher
An Wang Middle School
Lowell, Massachusetts

Stu Danzinger
Supervisor
Community Consolidated
School District 59
Arlington Heights, Illinois

Esther Draper
Supervisor/Science Specialist
Belair Math Science
Magnet School
Pine Bluff, Arkansas

Sue Esser
Teacher
Loretto Elementary
Jacksonville, Florida

Dr. Richard Fairman
Teacher
Antioch University
Yellow Springs, Ohio

Joan Goldfarb
Teacher
Indialantic Elementary
Indialantic, Florida

Deborah Gomes
Teacher
A J Gomes Elementary
New Bedford, Massachusetts

Sandy Hobart
Teacher
Mims Elementary
Mims, Florida

Tom Hocker
Teacher/Science Coach
Boston Latin Academy
Dorchester, Massachusetts

Shelley Jaques
Science Supervisor
Moore Public Schools
Moore, Oklahoma

Marguerite W. Jones
Teacher
Spearman Elementary
Piedmont, South Carolina

Kelly Kenney
Teacher
Kansas City Missouri
School District
Kansas City, Missouri

Carol Kilbane
Teacher
Riverside Elementary School
Wichita, Kansas

Robert Kolenda
Teacher
Neshaminy School District
Langhorne, Pennsylvania

Karen Lynn Kruse
Teacher
St. Paul the Apostle
Yonkers, New York

Elizabeth Loures
Teacher
Point Fermin
Elementary School
San Pedro, California

Susan MacDougall
Teacher
Brick Community Primary
Learning Center
Brick, New Jersey

Jack Marine
Teacher
Raising Horizons Quest
Charter School
Philadelphia, Pennsylvania

Nicola Micozzi Jr.
Science Coordinator
Plymouth Public Schools
Plymouth, Massachusetts

Paula Monteiro
Teacher
A J Gomes Elementary
New Bedford, Massachusetts

Tracy Newallis
Teacher
Taper Avenue Elementary
San Pedro, California

Dr. Eugene Nicolo
Supervisor, Science K-12
Moorestown School District
Moorestown, New Jersey

Jeffry Pastrak
School District of Philadelphia
Philadelphia, Pennslyvania

Helen Pedigo
Teacher
Mt. Carmel Elementary
Huntsville Alabama

Becky Peltonen
Teacher
Patterson Elementary School
Panama City, Florida

Sherri Pensler
Teacher/ESOL
Claude Pepper Elementary
Miami, Florida

Virginia Rogliano
Teacher
Bridgeview Elementary
South Charleston, West
Virginia

Debbie Sanders
Teacher
Thunderbolt Elementary
Orange Park, Florida

Grethel Santamarina
Teacher
E.W.F. Stirrup School
Miami, Florida

Migdalia Schneider
Teacher/Bilingual
Lindell School
Long Beach, New York

Susan Shelly
Teacher
Bonita Springs Elementary
Bonita Springs, Florida

Peggy Terry
Teacher
Madison Elementary
South Holland, Illinois

Jane M. Thompson
Teacher
Emma Ward Elementary
Lawrenceburg, Kentucky

Martha Todd
Teacher
W. H. Rhodes Elementary
Milton, Florida

Renee Williams
Teacher
Bloomfield Schools
Central Primary
Bloomfield, New Mexico

Myra Wood
Teacher
Madison Street Academy
Ocala, Florida

Marion Zampa
Teacher
Shawnee Mission
School District
Overland Park, Kansas

Science

See learning in a whole new light

Unit A Life Science

What do living things need?

Chapter 1 • Living and Nonliving

Chapter 2 • Habitats

Where do plants and animals live?

Unit A Life Science

How do parts help living things?

Chapter 3 • How Plants and Animals Live

Chapter 4 • Life Cycles

How do animals and plants grow and change?

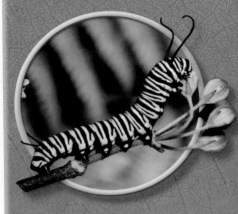

Unit A Life Science

How are living things connected?

Chapter 5 • Food Chains

Unit B Earth Science

How are land, water, and air important?

Chapter 6 • Land, Water, and Air

WE RECYCLE

Chapter 7 • Weather

What are the four seasons?

Unit C Physical Science

How can objects be described?

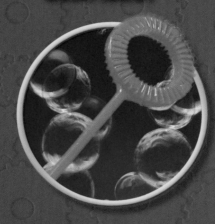

Chapter 8 • Observing Matter

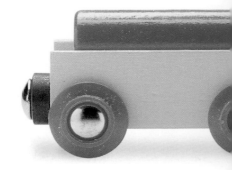

Chapter 9 • Movement and Sound

What makes objects move?

Unit C Physical Science

Where does energy come from?

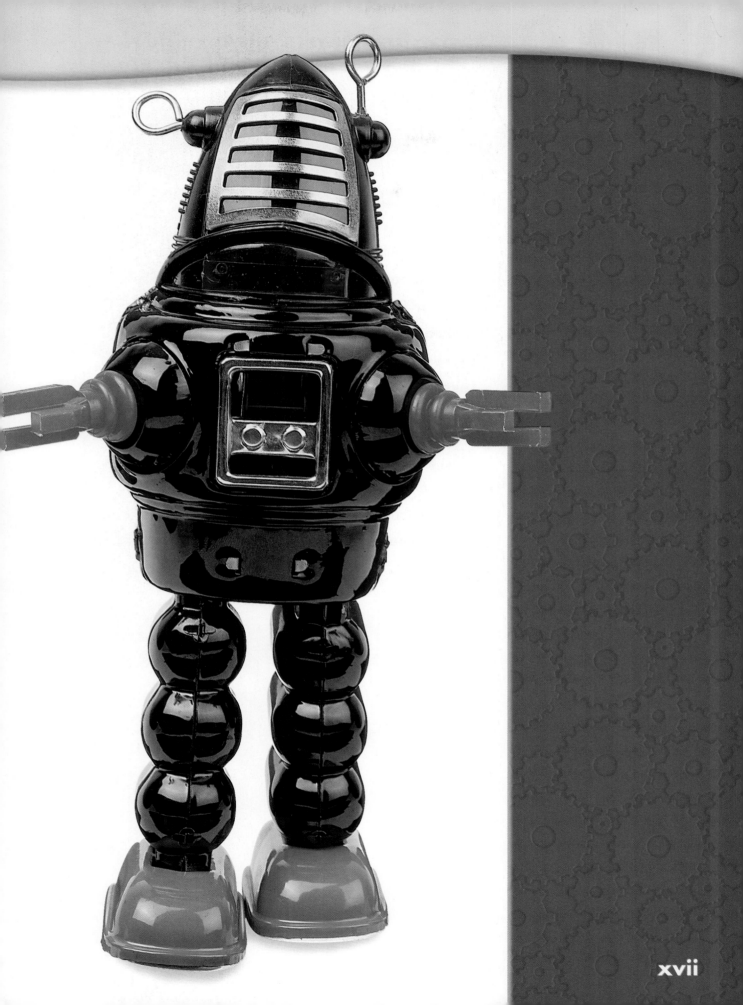

Unit D Space and Technology

What is in the sky?

Chapter 12 • Science in Our World

How does technology help people?

How to Read Science

Each chapter in your book has a page like this one.
This page shows you how to use a reading skill.

Before reading

First, read the Build Background page. Next, read the How To Read Science page. Then, think about what you already know. Last, make a list of what you already know.

Target Reading Skill

The target reading skill will help you understand what you read.

Real-World Connection

Each page has an example of something you will learn.

Graphic Organizer

A graphic organizer can help you think about what you learn.

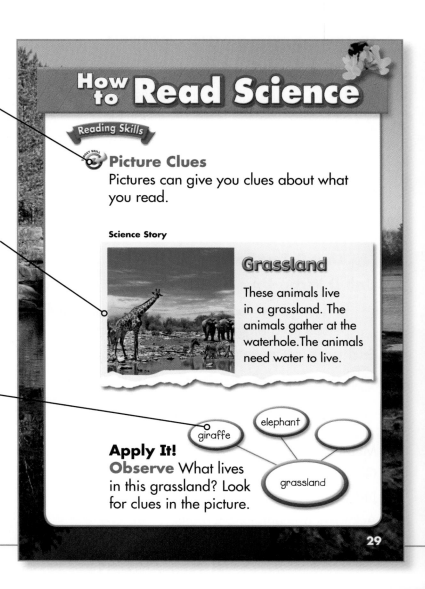

Map Facts
A swamp is a wetland. Okefenokee Swamp in Georgia has about 70 islands.

crane

dragonfly

bullfrog

✓ **Lesson Checkpoint**
1. What does a duck get in a wetland?
2. Use **picture clues** to tell what animals live in a wetland.

35

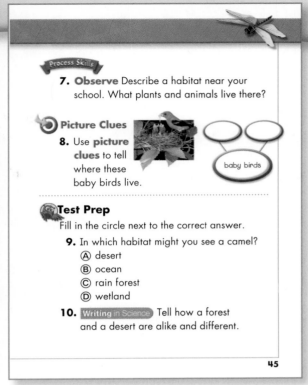

Process Skills

7. **Observe** Describe a habitat near your school. What plants and animals live there?

Picture Clues
8. Use **picture clues** to tell where these baby birds live.

baby birds

Test Prep
Fill in the circle next to the correct answer.
9. In which habitat might you see a camel?
   Ⓐ desert
   Ⓑ ocean
   Ⓒ rain forest
   Ⓓ wetland
10. Writing in Science Tell how a forest and a desert are alike and different.

45

During reading

Use the checkpoint as you read the lesson. This will help you check how much you understand.

After reading

Think about what you have learned. Compare what you learned with the list you made before you read the chapter. Answer the questions in the Chapter Review.

Target Reading Skills

These are some target reading skills that appear in this book.

- Cause and Effect
- Alike and Different
- Put Things in Order
- Predict

- Draw Conclusions
- Picture Clues
- Important Details

Science Process Skills

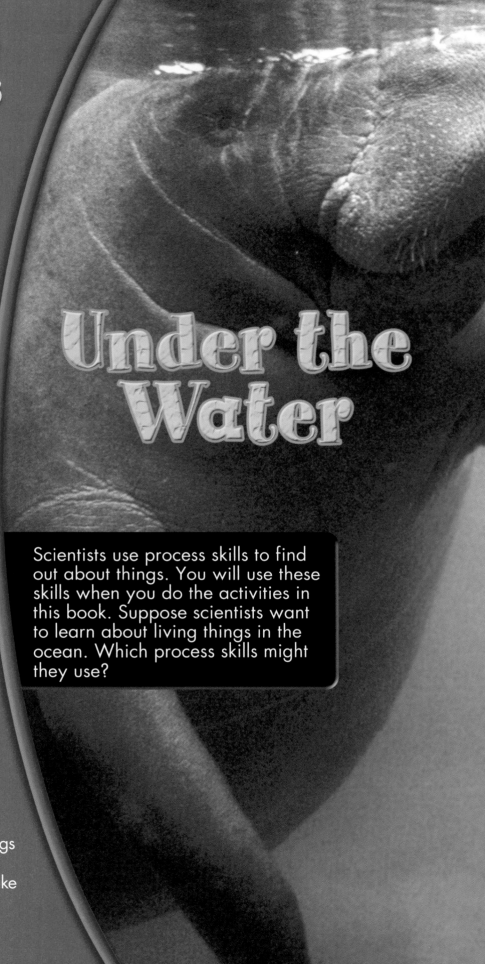

Under the Water

Observe
A scientist who wants to find out about the ocean observes many things. You use your senses to find out about things too.

Classify
Scientists classify living things in the ocean. You classify when you sort or group things by their properties.

Estimate and Measure
Scientists can estimate the size of living things in the ocean. This means they make a careful guess about the size or amount of something. Then they measure it.

Infer
Scientists are always learning about living things in the ocean. Scientists draw a conclusion or make a guess from what they already know.

Scientists use process skills to find out about things. You will use these skills when you do the activities in this book. Suppose scientists want to learn about living things in the ocean. Which process skills might they use?

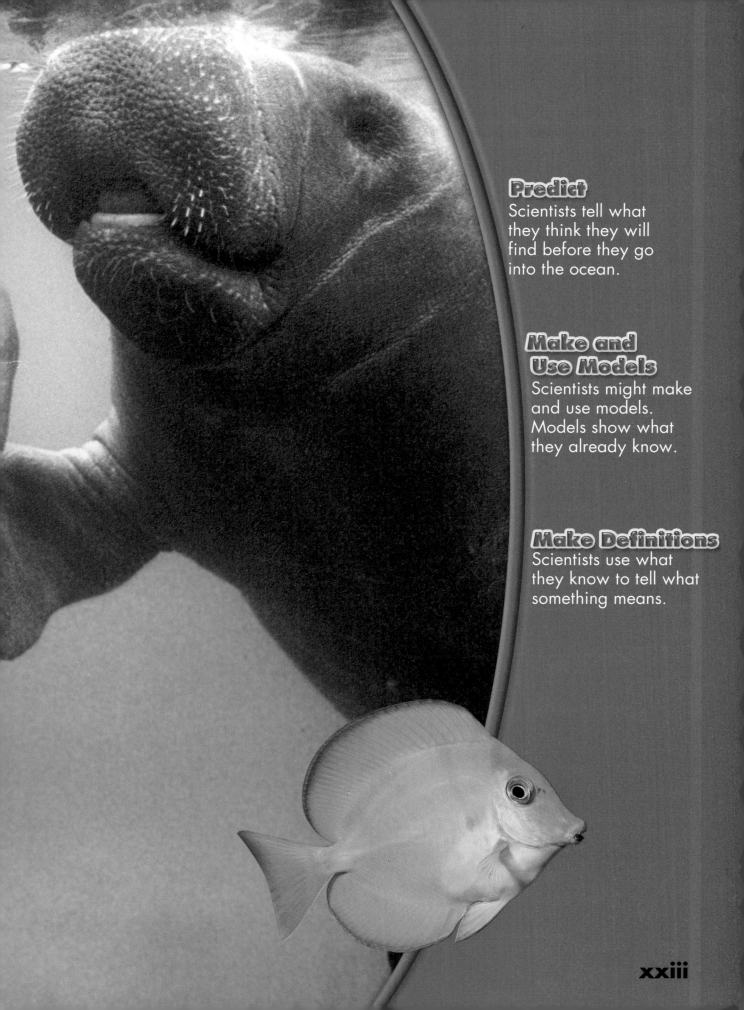

Predict
Scientists tell what they think they will find before they go into the ocean.

Make and Use Models
Scientists might make and use models. Models show what they already know.

Make Definitions
Scientists use what they know to tell what something means.

Science Process Skills

Make Hypotheses

Think of a question you have about living things in the ocean. Make a statement that you can test to answer your question.

Suppose you were a scientist. You might want to learn more about the ocean. What questions might you have? How would you use process skills to help you learn?

Collect Data

Scientists record what they observe and measure. Scientists put this data into charts or graphs.

Interpret Data

Scientists use what they learn to solve problems or answer questions.

Investigate and Experiment
Scientists plan and do an investigation as they study the ocean.

Control Variables
Scientists plan a fair test. Scientists change only one thing in their test. Scientists keep everything else the same.

Communicate
Scientists tell what they learn about living things in the ocean.

Using Scientific Methods

Scientific methods are ways of finding answers. Scientific methods have these steps. Sometimes scientists do the steps in a different order. Scientists do not always do all of the steps.

Ask a question.

Ask a question that you want answered.

Do seeds need water to grow?

Make your hypothesis.

Tell what you think the answer is to your question.

If seeds are watered, then they will grow.

Plan a fair test.

Change only one thing.

Keep everything else the same.

Water one pot with seeds.

no water

water

Do your test.

Test your hypothesis. Do your test more than once. See if your results are the same.

Collect and record your data.

Keep records of what you find out. Use words or drawings to help.

Tell your conclusion.

Observe the results of your test. Decide if your hypothesis is right or wrong. Tell what you decide.

Seeds need water to grow.

no water

water

Go further.

Use what you learn. Think of new questions or better ways to do a test.

Ask a Question

Make Your Hypothesis

Plan a Fair Test

Do Your Test

Collect and Record Your Data

Tell Your Conclusion

Go Further

Science Tools

Scientists use many different kinds of tools.

Measuring cup
You can use a measuring cup to measure volume. Volume is how much space something takes up.

Stopwatch
A stopwatch measures how much time something takes.

Computer
You can learn about science at a special Internet website. Go to www.pearsonsuccessnet.com.

Ruler
You can use a ruler to measure how long something is. Most scientists use a ruler to measure length in centimeters or millimeters.

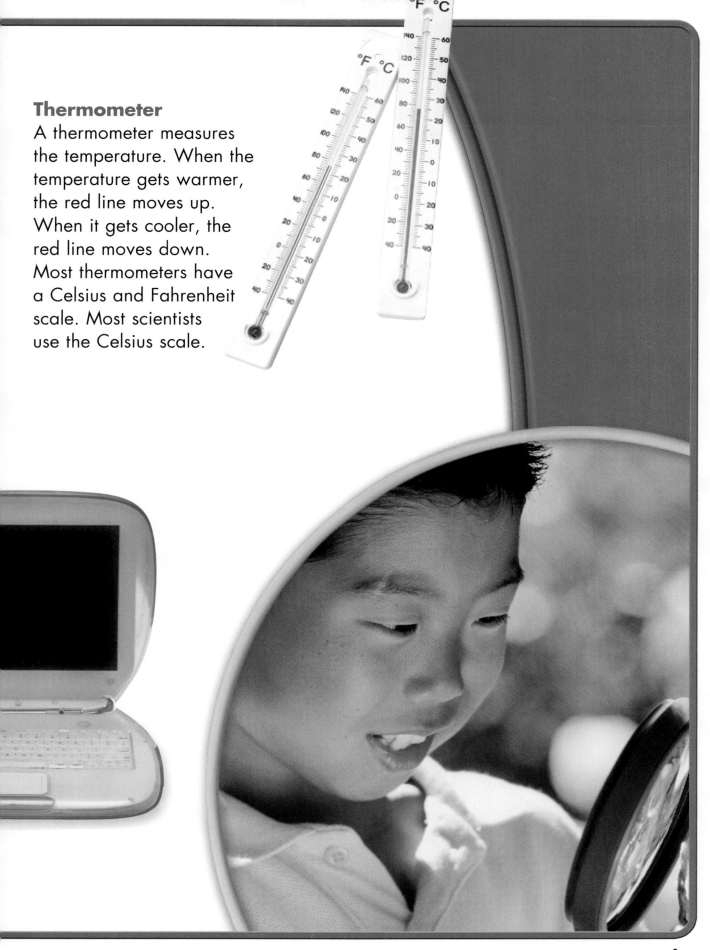

Thermometer

A thermometer measures the temperature. When the temperature gets warmer, the red line moves up. When it gets cooler, the red line moves down. Most thermometers have a Celsius and Fahrenheit scale. Most scientists use the Celsius scale.

Science Tools

Calculator

A calculator can help you do things, such as add and subtract.

Safety goggles

You can use safety goggles to protect your eyes.

Balance

A balance is used to measure the mass of objects. Mass is how much matter an object has. Most scientists measure mass in grams or kilograms.

Meterstick

You can use a meterstick to measure how long something is too. Scientists use a meterstick to measure in meters.

Clock

A clock measures time.

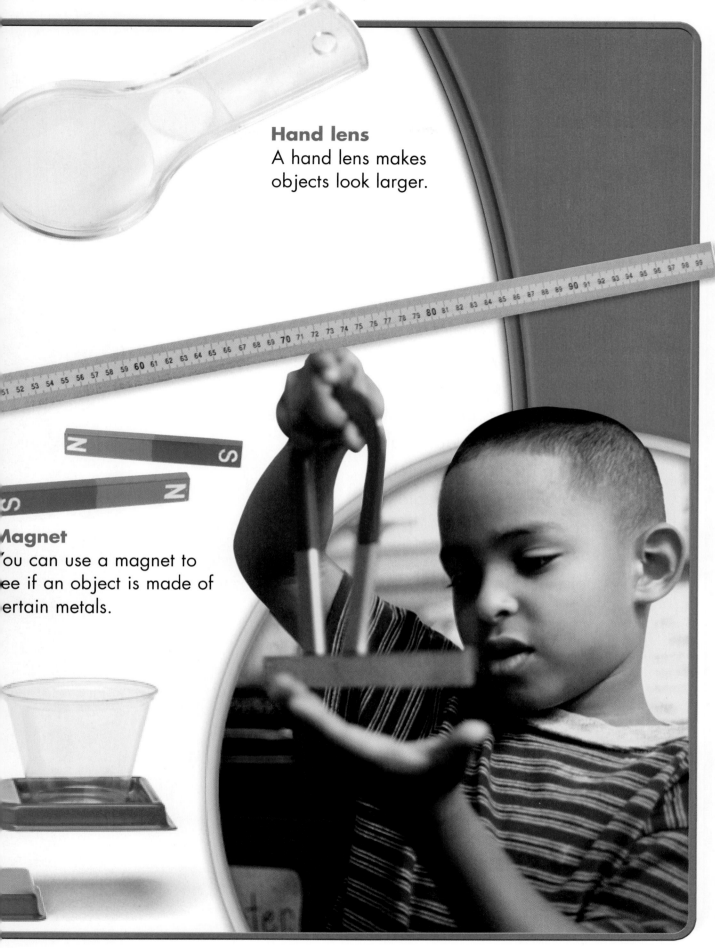

Hand lens
A hand lens makes objects look larger.

Magnet
You can use a magnet to see if an object is made of certain metals.

Safety in Science

You need to be careful when doing science activities. This page includes safety tips to remember:

- Listen to your teacher's instructions.
- Never taste or smell materials unless your teacher tells you to.
- Wear safety goggles when needed.
- Handle scissors and other equipment carefully.
- Keep your work place neat and clean.
- Clean up spills immediately.
- Tell your teacher immediately about accidents or if you see something that looks unsafe.
- Wash your hands well after every activity.

Chapter 11
Day and Night Sky

You Will Discover

- what causes day and night.
- why the Moon looks different every night.

online
Student Edition
pearsonsuccessnet.com

What is in the sky?

Sun

star

rotation

Moon

planet

telescope

315

Explore Why does the Sun look small?

Materials

ruler

paper plate

What to Do

1 Measure across a plate. Label the plate **Sun**.

2 Have your partner hold the plate.

3 Move 5 steps away from your partner.

4 Hold the ruler in front of you. Close one eye. Measure again.

Sun

Process Skills

You can **communicate** how the size of the plate seems to change.

Explain Your Results

Communicate What seems to happen to the size of the plate when you move away?

How to Read Science

 TARGET SKILL

Important Details
Important details are pictures and words that tell you something.

Science Story

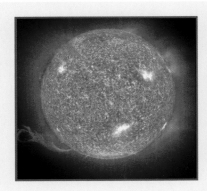

The Sun

We get light from the Sun. The Sun is very far from Earth. You can see the Sun in the day sky.

Apply It!
Communicate List three important details you saw and read about the Sun.

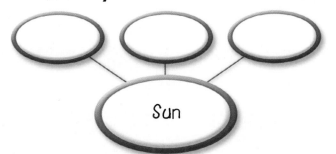

Sun

317

Look Up High!

Sung to the tune of "This Old Man"
Lyrics by Gerri Brioso & Richard Freitas/The Dovetail Group, Inc.

The daytime sky, the daytime sky.

What do you see in the daytime sky?

Please look up and tell me
   everything you see,

In the sky above you and me.

Science Songs

Lesson 1

What is in the day sky?

You can see the Sun in the day sky. The **Sun** is a star. A **star** is a big ball of hot gas.

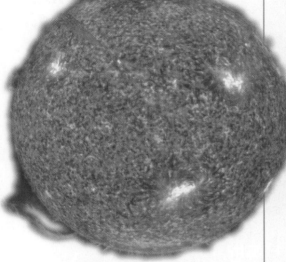

The Sun makes the day sky bright.

What else do you see in the day sky? You may see clouds. You may see birds.

Sometimes you can even see the Moon in the day sky.

The Sun is low in the sky early in the day.

The Sun is above you at noon.

The Sun warms the baby lion.

Plants need sunlight to grow.

The Bright Sun

The Sun lights Earth. Living things need light from the Sun to live and grow.

The Sun is bigger than Earth. The Sun looks small because it is far away.

**The Sun is low in the sky
again late in the day.**

We say that the Sun rises and
sets, but really it does not.
The Sun looks like it is moving
because Earth is moving.

✓ **Lesson Checkpoint**

1. Why does the Sun look small?

2. **Writing** in Science Write in your
   science journal. Tell about
   the Sun.

What causes day and night?

Earth is always moving.
Earth turns around and around.
This is called **rotation.**
Earth makes one rotation every day.

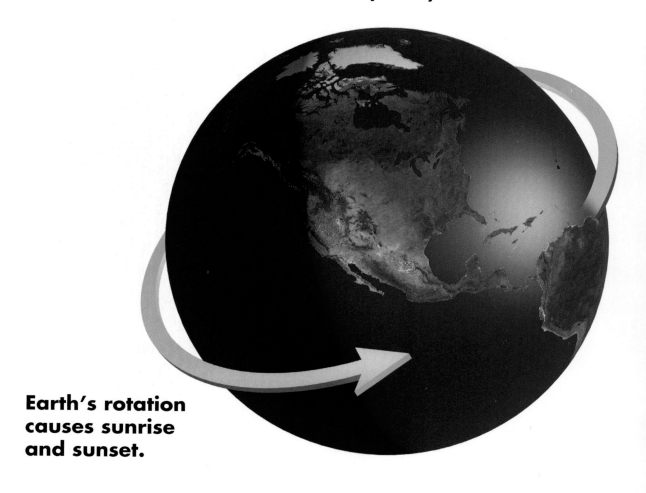

Earth's rotation causes sunrise and sunset.

It is night when your part of Earth faces away from the Sun.

It is day when your part of Earth faces the Sun. Earth's rotation causes day and night.

It is night in Tokyo when it is day in Chicago.

It is day in Chicago when it is night in Tokyo.

✓ **Lesson Checkpoint**

1. How often does Earth make one rotation?

2. **Math in Science** What comes next in the pattern below?
day, night, day, night, day, _____

What is in the night sky?

You may see stars in the night sky.
Stars give off light.
Stars seem to move across the night sky.

Earth is a **planet.**
Planets do not give off light.
Planets move around the Sun.

You might use a telescope
to see things in the sky.
A **telescope** makes things
that are far away look closer.

A telescope makes things look bigger or brighter.

Stars look tiny because they are far away. The Sun is the closest star to Earth.

Saturn, Mars, and Venus are planets. Sometimes you can see these planets in the night sky.

1. ✓Checkpoint How does a telescope help us look at things in the sky?

2. 🎯 **Important Details** Name planets you might see in the night sky.

The Moon at Night

The **Moon** moves around Earth. The Moon looks small because it is far away.

The Moon is round.

The Moon is not like Earth.
The Moon has no air.
The Moon has no animals.
The Moon has no plants.

This is what the Moon looks like at different times.

The Sun's light shines on the Moon. You only see the part of the Moon lit by the Sun.

The part of the moon lit by the Sun changes each night. The Moon looks a little different each night. The Moon looks the same again about every 29 days.

> ✔ **Lesson Checkpoint**
> 1. How long does it take for the Moon to look the same again?
> 2. ↻ What is one **important detail** you saw or read about the Moon?

Investigate Why can you see things in the night sky?

Materials

shoe box viewer

star and ball

flashlight

clay

What to Do

1 **Make a model** of the night sky.

2 Put the star in the clay. Put the lid on the box. Observe.

Look through this hole.

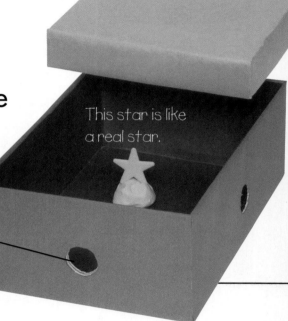

This star is like a real star.

3 Take out the star. Put the ball on the clay. Put the lid on the box.

The ball is like the Moon.

Look through this hole.

Process Skills

Investigate to learn why you can see things in the night sky.

4 Shine the flashlight through the side hole. Observe.

The flashlight is like the Sun.

Look through this hole.

	Did you need a flashlight to see it? yes or no
Ball	
Star	

Explain Your Results

1. Why can you see the star in the dark?

2. **Infer** Why can you see the Moon in the night sky?

Go Further

How could you show that the Moon can sometimes be seen in the day sky? **Investigate** to find out.

Reading a Calendar

This calendar shows how the Moon looks at different times of the month.

May

Sunday	Monday	Tuesday	Wednesday	Thursday	Friday	Saturday
				New Moon **1**	**2**	**3**
4	**5**	**6**	**7**	First quarter **8**	**9**	**10**
11	**12**	**13**	**14**	Full Moon **15**	**16**	**17**
18	**19**	**20**	**21**	**22**	Third Quarter **23**	**24**
25	**26**	**27**	**28**	**29**	New Moon **30**	**31**

Use the calendar to answer the questions.
1. How many days are there from the new Moon to the first quarter Moon?
2. How many days are there from the new Moon to the full Moon?

Lab zone Take-Home Activity

Look for the Moon in the sky tonight. Estimate how many days until there will be a new Moon.

Vocabulary

Which picture goes with each word?

1. Moon
2. Sun
3. telescope
4. planet

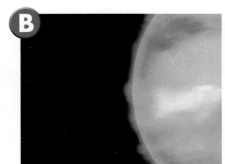

What did you learn?

5. What causes night and day?

6. What can you see in the night sky?

7. How does a telescope help you see the Moon?

The Moon

The Moon is in the night sky. Part of the Moon is lit by the Sun's light.

Process Skills

8. Infer Why does it feel cooler on Earth when there are many clouds in the sky?

Important Details

9. List two **important details** you saw or read about the Moon.

Moon

Test Prep

Fill in the circle next to the correct answer.

10. Which of these gives off light?

(A) the Moon

(B) Earth

(C) a planet

(D) a star

11. Writing in Science Think about Earth and the Moon. Write how they are alike and different.

NASA Exploring the Sky

A time line shows when things happened. Look at this time line.

1960   1970   1980

1962
Friendship 7

1973
Skylab began.

1969
Apollo 11

1981
Space Shuttle *Columbia* makes first flight.

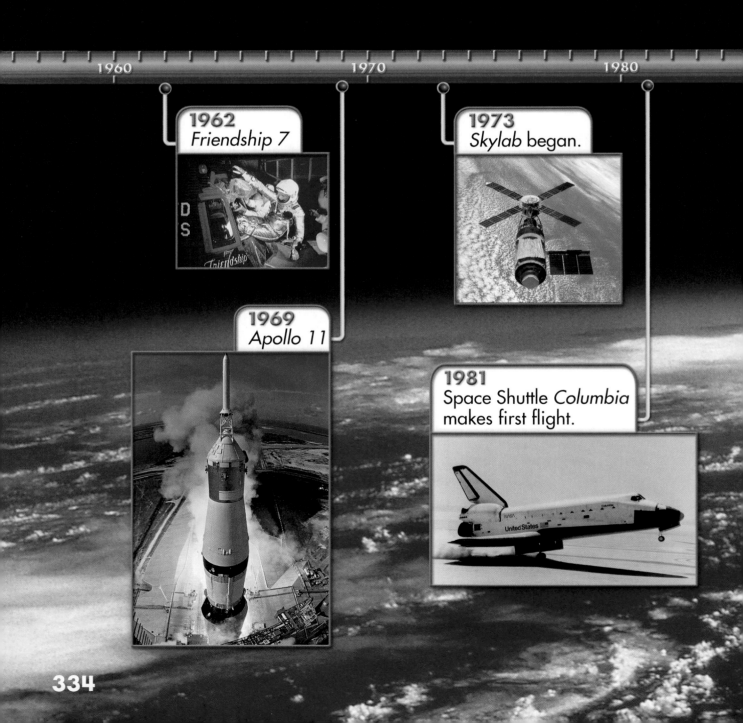

The pictures on these two pages show ways that NASA learns about space. These machines help NASA get information about space. These machines help NASA do experiments.

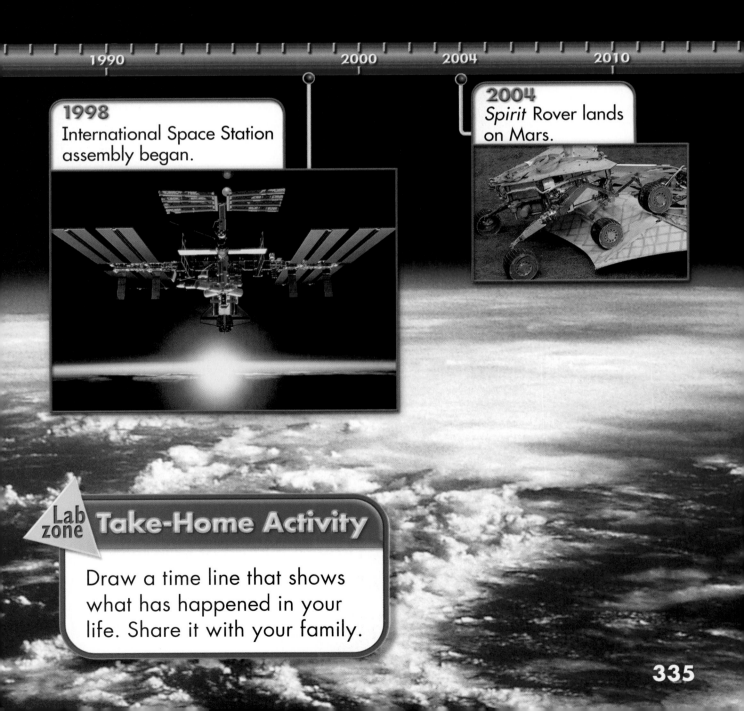

1990   2000   2004   2010

1998
International Space Station assembly began.

2004
Spirit Rover lands on Mars.

Lab zone Take-Home Activity

Draw a time line that shows what has happened in your life. Share it with your family.

Career

Astronauts

Read Together

Astronauts go into space in space shuttles.
Astronauts do work in space.
Astonauts do science experiments in space.
Astronauts fix things in space.
Astronauts take pictures in space. Astronauts need special training to work in space.

Stephanie Wilson is an astronaut. She is a mission specialist with NASA.

Lab zone ▶ Take-Home Activity

Draw a picture of yourself as an astronaut working in space. Tell what kind of work you might do in space.

Chapter 12
Science in Our World

Discovery Channel School
Student DVD
DISCOVERY CHANNEL SCHOOL

online
Student Edition
pearsonsuccessnet.com

You Will Discover

- what tools and machines are used to farm and build.
- that tools and machines are used to communicate.

How does technology help people?

technology

simple machine

wheel and axle

wedge

Chapter 12 Vocabulary

inclined plane

pulley

screw

lever

Explore How can you use tools?

A tool can help you do a task.

Materials

4 blocks

tools

What to Do

1 Use tools to stack blocks. Do not touch the blocks.

2 Try using different tools.

Explain Your Results

Communicate Tell how you used the tools. Draw what you did first, next, and last.

Put Things in Order

You tell what happens first, next, then, and last when you put things in order.

Science Diagram

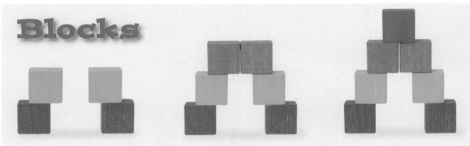

Blocks

Sara built a block tower. First, she put two blue blocks on a table. Next, she put two yellow blocks on top of the blue blocks. Then, she put two green blocks on top of the yellow blocks. Last, she put an orange block on top.

Apply It!

Communicate Tell which blocks come first, next, then, and last.

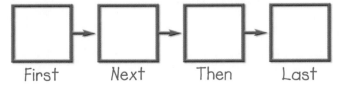

First   Next   Then   Last

Technology Helps

Sung to the tune of "On Top of Old Smokey"
Lyrics by Gerri Brioso & Richard Freitas/The Dovetail Group, Inc.

Technology helps all
The farmers I know,
To make their work easier
Than a long time ago.

Science Songs

How do farmers use technology to grow food?

Some food comes from lakes or oceans. Some food comes from the land. Farmers grow some food.

Machines help farmers grow food. Machines are one kind of technology. **Technology** is the use of scientific knowledge to solve problems.

Farmers use machines to grow wheat. Wheat is used to make bread.

Planting and Growing Corn

It is time to plant corn!
The farmer uses a plow to get
the soil ready for planting.
The plow makes the work easier.
The plow makes the work take
less time.

The plow turns the soil.

The farmer uses a seed drill to plant corn seeds. The seed drill makes the work go fast. Soon all of the corn seeds are planted. Corn plants begin to grow.

A seed drill machine helps plant corn.

✔️ Lesson Checkpoint

1. How does a plow help a farmer plant corn?

2. Writing in Science Make a list of foods you eat that come from a farm.

How does food get from the farm to the store?

The farmer checks the corn. The farmer will pick the corn when it is ready.

First, the corn seeds grow into a corn plant.

Next, the farmer checks the corn.

The farmer uses a harvester machine to pick the corn. The corn is loaded into a truck. The truck takes the corn to the store.

✓ **Lesson Checkpoint**

1. Name two machines used to get corn from the farm to the store.

2. 🎯 **Put Things in Order** Tell how corn gets from a field to your home.

Then, the farmer uses a machine to pick the corn.

Last, you might buy the corn at the store.

Lesson 3

What tools can you use to make dinner?

People use tools to make work easier. Each tool helps do a different job. Only use a knife or scissors when an older person can help you.

Cut! Cut!

Scissors can help you cut tortillas for chips.

A grater can help you cut cheese into small pieces.

A measuring cup can help you get the right amount of cheese.

What other tools might you use to make tacos and salsa for dinner?

A big spoon can help you stir the salsa.

A strainer can help you dry the wet lettuce.

A knife can help cut corn from the cob.

1. ✔Checkpoint What tools might be used to make dinner?

2. **Math** in Science You used 4 big spoons. You used 5 small spoons. How many spoons did you use?

Serving Dinner

It is dinner time! What tools do you need to serve the tacos and salsa?

A large spoon can help you lift the meat.

Tongs can help you pick up the lettuce.

Always have an older person help you when something is hot. A trivet keeps the hot pot from burning the table.

A ladle is a big, deep spoon. A ladle can help you get some salsa.

A spatula can help you lift hot tortillas off the pan.

✓ **Lesson Checkpoint**

1. What are three tools you can use to serve dinner?

2. **Technology** in Science Draw a tool you use in the kitchen. Tell how it helps you do work.

How do builders get wood for a house?

Technology changes over time.

Long ago loggers used an ax to cut down trees. Now loggers use a machine called a tree shears to cut down trees.

A tree shears makes cutting trees easier.

The logs are heavy. Long ago some loggers used animals to move the logs. Now loggers use a grappler to move the logs.

1. ✓ Checkpoint What machine does a logger use to cut down trees today?

2. Technology in Science How does a grappler help loggers?

A grappler makes moving logs easier.

353

Moving Logs to the Sawmill

The heavy logs need to be loaded onto the truck.

The long-armed knuckle boom machine grabs the heavy logs. Then the machine loads the logs onto the truck.

First, the long-armed knuckle boom loads the logs onto the truck.

Next, the truck takes the logs to the sawmill.

When the truck is full, it takes
the logs to the sawmill.

The logs are made into boards when
they arrive at the sawmill.

✓ **Lesson Checkpoint**

1. Tell what happens at a sawmill.

2. 🎯 **Put Things in Order** Tell how
a tree gets from the forest to a sawmill.

**Then, another
machine takes the
bark off the logs.**

**Last, the logs are cut
into boards. Now a
builder can use them
to build a house.**

Lesson 5

What are simple machines?

A **simple machine** is a tool with few or no moving parts that makes work easier.

A wedge is a simple machine. A **wedge** is used to push things apart.

A wheel and axle is a simple machine. A **wheel and axle** is used to move things.

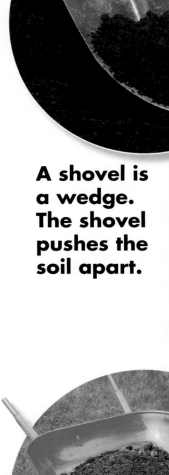

A shovel is a wedge. The shovel pushes the soil apart.

A wheelbarrow has a wheel and axle.

SciLinks Take It to the Net
pearsonsuccessnet.com   keyword: simple machine
                         code: g1p356

Builders use many simple machines to make work easier.

1. ✔Checkpoint How do simple machines help people?

2. Technology in Science What are some machines that have a wheel and axle?

Using Simple Machines

A screw is a simple machine.
A **screw** is used to hold
things together.

A lever is a simple machine.
A **lever** can be used to
lift something.

A pulley is a simple machine.
A **pulley** uses a wheel
and rope to move things up
and down.

Screws
hold wood
boards
together.

A lever helps lift th
nail from the boar

Builders use a pull
to move objects.

An inclined plane helps to move things up or down.

An inclined plane is a simple machine. An **inclined plane** is high at one end and low at the other end.

☑ **Lesson Checkpoint**

1. What three simple machines can help lift things or move things up?

2. **Writing in Science** Write in your **science journal.** Tell about two simple machines that help people.

Lesson 6

What can you use to communicate?

People use technology to communicate every day.

We use technology to take pictures, listen to the radio, and help other people.

What are some ways you use technology to communicate with other people?

Hurry!
Computers tell the firefighters where to go.

Click!
You can use a digital camera. You can use email to send the picture to a friend.

Are you at the baseball game? No, you can listen to the baseball game on a radio!

✓ Lesson Checkpoint

1. How do a camera and email help you communicate?

2. Social Studies in Science How can you use technology to hear news about people who live far away from you?

Investigate How can you build a strong bridge?

Materials

safety goggles

4 books and a ruler

10 stir sticks and 10 craft sticks

tape and note card

cup and pennies

Process Skills

Making a model can help you understand why some bridges are stronger than others.

What to Do

1 Place the books 25 centimeters apart.

Wear your goggles.

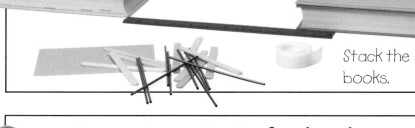

Stack the books.

2 **Make a model** of a bridge using stir sticks and a note card.

3 Place the bridge between the books. Place the cup on the bridge.

4 **Estimate** how many pennies the bridge will hold. Record.

5 Put pennies in the cup one at a time. How many pennies did the bridge hold before it fell? Record.

Which bridge is stronger?

	Number of Pennies	
	Estimate	Count
Stir Sticks		
Craft Sticks		

6 Try it again. Use craft sticks.

Explain Your Results

1. How are your **models** like real bridges?

2. Explain why one bridge held more pennies than the other bridge.

Go Further

What would happen if you put the books closer together? Make a model to find the answer.

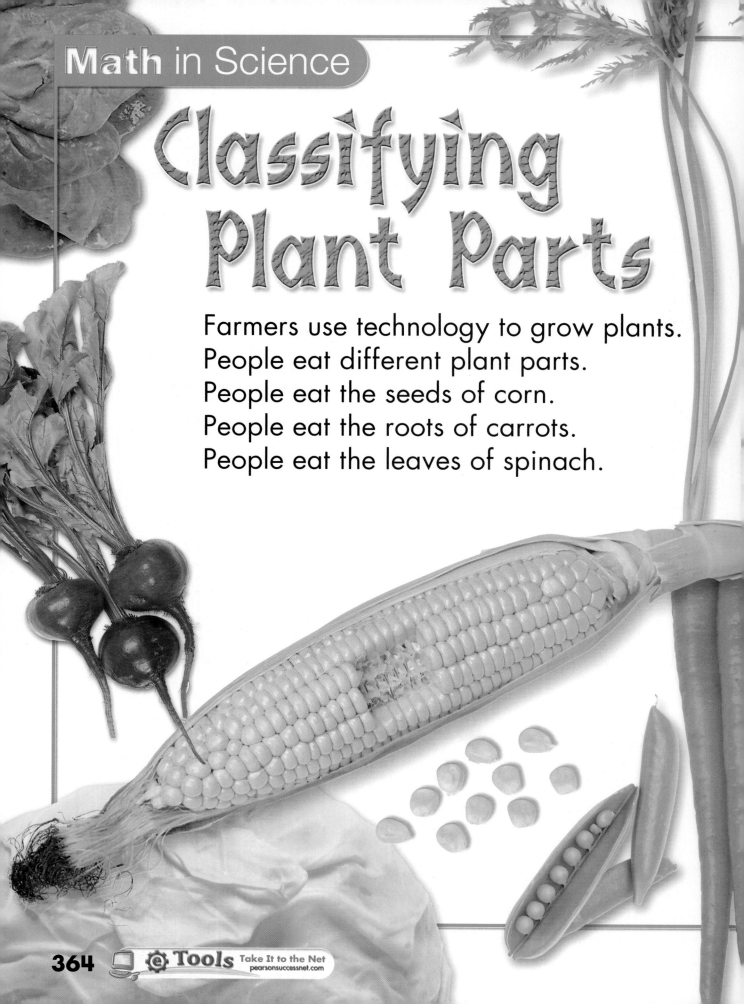

Classifying Plant Parts

Farmers use technology to grow plants.
People eat different plant parts.
People eat the seeds of corn.
People eat the roots of carrots.
People eat the leaves of spinach.

eTools Take It to the Net
pearsonsuccessnet.com

Plant Parts People Eat

Seeds	Roots	Leaves
corn	carrots	spinach
peas	beets	cabbage
lima beans	radishes	
	turnips	

Use the chart to answer these questions.
1. Does this chart show more kinds of plant seeds or plant roots that people eat?
2. Which part of a radish do people eat?

Lab zone Take-Home Activity

Make a chart like the one on this page. Draw one plant seed that you eat. Draw one plant root that you eat. Draw two plant leaves that you eat.

Vocabulary

Which picture goes with each word?

1. wheel and axle
2. wedge
3. inclined plane
4. screw
5. lever
6. pulley

What did you learn?

7. What is technology?

8. List three tools you might use to make dinner. Tell how you could use each tool.

9. List three machines used to get wood. Tell how the machines are used.

10. Communicate What is a simple machine?

Put Things in Order

11. Look at the pictures. Tell which one comes first, next, then, and last.

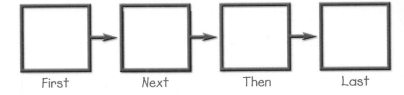

| First | → | Next | → | Then | → | Last |

Test Prep

Fill in the circle next to the correct answer.

12. Where are logs cut into boards?

Ⓐ farm

Ⓑ kitchen

Ⓒ sawmill

Ⓓ forest

13. Writing in Science Write a story about two friends that use technology to communicate.

Mike Wong

Read Together

Mike Wong liked to make paper airplanes as a child. His room was full of paper airplanes. He wanted to know how airplanes flew.

Now Mike Wong works at NASA. He uses computers to find out what aircraft shapes are the best for flying. People at NASA use what they learn from Mr. Wong to make better aircraft.

Mike Wong is an aeronautical engineer.

Lab zone Take-Home Activity

Make a paper airplane. Measure how far your paper airplane can fly.

Test-Taking Strategies

Find Important Words

Choose the Right Answer

Use Information from Text and Graphics

▶ Write Your Answer

Write Your Answer

Read the story.

Sunlight

Sunlight is important to living things on Earth. Sunlight gives heat and light to Earth. Sunlight helps plants grow.

Read the question.

Why is the Sun important to living things on Earth?

Which words help you to write your answer? Write your answer.

369

Unit D Wrap-Up

Chapter 11

What is in the sky?
- The Sun and the Moon are in the sky.
- Stars and planets are in the sky.

Chapter 12

How does technology help people?
- Technology helps farmers grow crops.
- Technology helps people build buildings.
- Technology helps people communicate.

Performance Assessment

Make a Tool That Will Help You Work

- Make a tool that can carry things.
- Tell how your tool would make work easier.

Read More About Space and Technology!

Look for books like these in your library.

Man On The Moon
by Anastasia Suen
illustrated by Benrei Huang

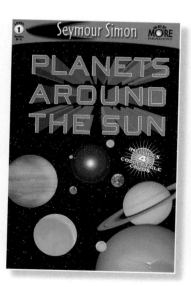

Seymour Simon
PLANETS AROUND THE SUN

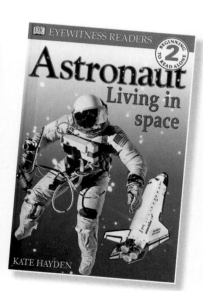

EYEWITNESS READERS
Astronaut
Living in space
KATE HAYDEN

Experiment How can a smaller person lift a bigger person on a seesaw?

A seesaw is a kind of lever. A smaller person can lift a bigger person on a seesaw. How can this happen? Experiment to find out.

Materials

eraser

ruler with cups

toy car

pennies

Process Skills

You use a **model** to find out how a seesaw moves.

Ask a question.
How can a smaller person lift a bigger person on a seesaw? Use a **model** to find out.

Make a hypothesis.
Does moving one cup closer to the middle change the number of pennies you need to lift the cup? Tell what you think.

Plan a fair test.
Make sure your cups are the same size.

Do your test.

1 Put the eraser under the ruler and cups. Put the toy in cup 1.

2 Add pennies to cup 2 until cup 1 lifts up. Record how many pennies you need.

3 Take the pennies out of the cup.

4 Move cup 1 closer to the middle.

Put the eraser in the middle.

5 Add pennies to cup 2 until cup 1 lifts up. Record how many pennies you need.

Collect and record data.

_____ pennies

_____ pennies

Tell your conclusion.
When did you use fewer pennies to lift cup 1? How can a smaller person lift a bigger person on a seesaw?

Go Further
What would happen if you added more pennies? Experiment to find out.

Taking Off

The airplane taxis down the field
And heads into the breeze,
It lifts its wheels above the ground,
It skims above the trees,

It rises higher and higher
Away up toward the sun,
It's just a speck against the sky
—And now it's gone!

Science Fair Projects

Full Inquiry

Using Scientific Methods
1. Ask a question.
2. Make a hypothesis.
3. Plan a fair test.
4. Do your test.
5. Record and collect data.
6. Tell your conclusion.
7. Go further.

Idea 1

Making Paper Airplanes

Plan a project.

Find out how changing the shape of a paper airplane may change how far it flies.

Idea 2

Changing a Wheel

Plan a project.
Find out how changing the size of the wagon's wheels may improve how the wagon rolls.

Metric and Customary Measurement

Science uses the metric system to measure things. Metric measurement is used around the world. Here is how different metric measurements compare to customary measurement.

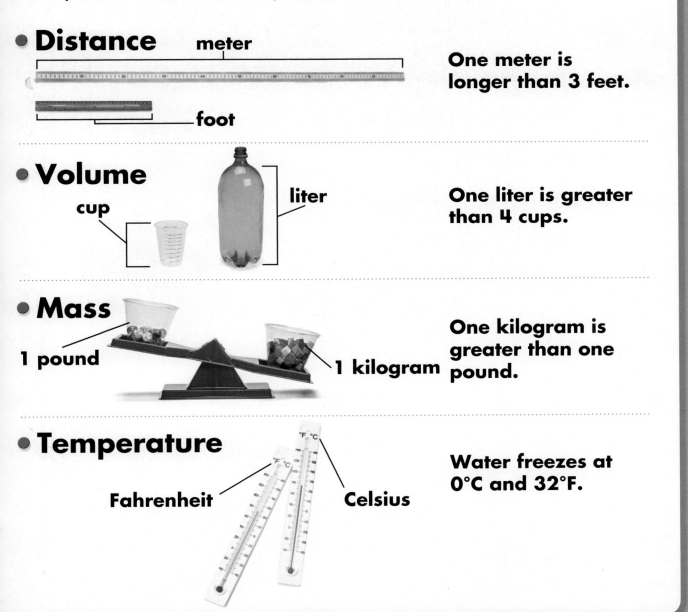

• Distance

meter

foot

One meter is longer than 3 feet.

• Volume

cup

liter

One liter is greater than 4 cups.

• Mass

1 pound

1 kilogram

One kilogram is greater than one pound.

• Temperature

Fahrenheit

Celsius

Water freezes at 0°C and 32°F.

Glossary

The glossary uses letters and signs to show how words are pronounced. The mark ′ is placed after a syllable with a primary or heavy accent. The mark ′ is placed after a syllable with a secondary or lighter accent.

To hear these words pronounced, listen to the AudioText CD.

alike (ə līk′) How things are the same. The two foxes look **alike**. (pages 5, 53, 96, 213)

antennae (an ten′ē) Feelers that help some animals know what is around them. **Antennae** help the crab feel, smell, and taste. (page 56)

Antennae

attract (ə trakt′) Attract means to pull toward. Magnets **attract** some objects. (page 256)

battery (bat′ər ē) Something that stores energy. The toy robot uses a **battery** to move. (page 293)

C

camouflage (kam′ə fläzh) A color or shape that makes an animal or plant hard to see. **Camouflage** helps the rabbit stay safe in its environment. (page 62)

cause (kȯz) Why something happens. Taking out the bottom block can cause the tower to fall. (pages 245, 254)

clay (klā) A soft part of soil that looks like mud, is sticky when wet, and is hard when dry. The **clay** felt sticky when Tanya touched it. (page 156)

cloud (kloud) A form in the air made of many tiny drops of water or pieces of ice when water vapor cools. We watched the fluffy, white **clouds** float overhead. (page 186)

desert (dez′ərt) A desert is a very dry habitat that gets little rain. Many **deserts** are hot during the day. (page 38)

different (dif′ər ənt) How things are not the same. The dogs are different colors. (pages 5, 53, 96, 213)

dissolve (di zolv′) To spread throughout a liquid. Salt will **dissolve** in water. (page 225)

draw conclusions

(drȯ kən klü′zhənz) When you decide something about what you see or read. You can **draw** a **conclusion** about what the shark will eat. (pages 117, 277)

E

effect (ə fekt′) What happens. The **effect** of pulling out the bottom block was that the blocks fell down. (pages 245, 254)

electricity (i lek′tris′ə tē) Makes things work. The streetlight uses **electricity** to shine. (page 290)

energy (en′ər jē) Something that can change things. Sunlight is a form of **energy** from the Sun. (page 282)

erosion (i rō′zhən) Happens when wind or water moves rocks and soil from one place to another. **Erosion** washed away the soil near the stream. (page 158)

evaporate (i vap′ə rāt′) To change from a liquid to a gas. The water on the ground quickly **evaporated** when the Sun came out. (page 228)

F

flower (flou′ər) The part of a plant that makes seeds. Our garden has many colorful **flowers**. (page 69)

food chain (füd chān) The way food passes from one living thing to another. All living things are connected through **food chains.** (page 125)

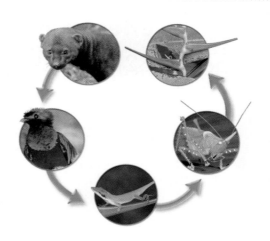

force (fôrs) A push or pull that makes objects move. The children used **force** to move the sled. (page 247)

forest (fôr′ist) A habitat with many trees and other types of plants. Many animals live in the **forest**. (page 31)

fuel (fyü′əl) Anything that is burned to make heat or power. People use gasoline as a **fuel** for cars. (page 290)

G

gas (gas) A kind of matter that can change size and shape. The bubbles are full of **gas**. (page 221)

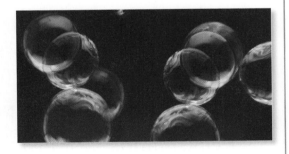

gravity (grav′ə tē) A force that pulls things toward the ground. **Gravity** pulls falling leaves toward the ground. (page 247)

habitat (hab′ə tat) A place where plants and animals live. A deer lives in a forest **habitat**. (page 31)

heat (hēt) Moves from warmer places and objects to cooler places and objects. The **heat** from the campfire kept us warm. (page 279)

humus (hyü′ məs) A nonliving material made up of parts of living things that have died. Grandmother adds **humus** to the soil to help her plants grow. (page 156)

important details (im pôrt′nt
di tālz′) Pictures and words that
tell you about something. We
looked for **important details**
in the book we were reading.
(pages 149, 317)

inclined plane (in klīnd′ plān)
A simple machine that is high at
one end and low at the other. It
helps move things up and down.
The builders used an **inclined
plane** to help move the wood.
(page 359)

larva (lär′və) A young insect that
has a different shape from the
adult. A butterfly **larva** is called
a caterpillar. (page 92)

leaf (lēf) A part of a plant that makes food for the plant. A **leaf** fell from the rose bush. (page 69)

lever (lev′ər) A simple machine that can be used to lift something. Denny used a **lever** to lift the nail out. (page 358)

life cycle (līf sī′kəl) The changes that take place as a plant or an animal grows and changes. The **life cycle** of a frog includes an egg, a tadpole, and a grown frog. (page 90)

liquid (lik′wid) Matter that takes the shape of its container. Water is a **liquid**. (page 220)

living (liv′ing) Things that are alive and can grow and change. The butterfly is a **living** thing. (page 7)

M

magnet (mag′nit) An object that attracts some kinds of metal. A **magnet** can pull an object made of iron without touching it. (pages 256, 258)

marsh (märsh) A wetland habitat. Many different plants and animals live in a **marsh**. (page 126)

mass (mas) Amount of matter in an object. Everything made of matter has **mass**. (page 215)

matter (mat′er) Anything that takes up space. Everything around you is made of **matter**. (page 215)

mineral (min′ər əl) A nonliving material that can be found in rocks and soil. Copper is a **mineral**. (page 164)

Moon (mün) An object in the sky that moves around Earth. The **Moon** was shining brightly in the night sky. (page 326)

natural resource

(nach′ər əl ri sôrs′) A useful thing that comes from nature. Rocks are a **natural resource**. (page 155)

nonliving (non liv′ing) Things that are not alive, don't grow, and don't change on their own. Tables and chairs are **nonliving** things. (page 14)

ocean (ō′shən) A large, deep habitat that has salt water. Some fish live in an **ocean** habitat. (page 36)

oxygen (ok′sə jən) A gas in the air that plants and animals need to live. Most living things need **oxygen** to live. (page 121)

planet (plan′it) A large body of matter that moves around the Sun. Earth is a **planet**. (page 324)

pole (pōl) At the end of some magnets. The north **pole** of one magnet will attract the south **pole** of another magnet. (page 256)

predict (pri dikt′) To make a guess from what you already know. See the clouds high in the sky. What do you **predict** the weather will be like? (page 181)

pulley (pul′ē) A simple machine that uses a wheel and rope to move things up and down. The workers used a **pulley** to move the wood. (page 358)

pupa (pyü′pə) The step after larva in some insects' life cycle. The hard covering of the **pupa** protects the caterpillar while it changes into a butterfly. (page 92)

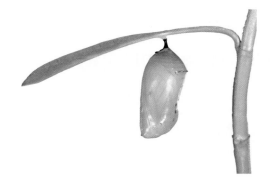

R

rain forest (rān fôr′ist) A habitat that gets a lot of rain. Plants with large green leaves grow in the **rain forest**. (page 122)

repel (ri pel′) To push away. The north poles of two magnets placed together will **repel** each other. (page 257)

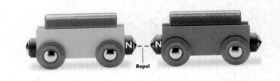

rocks (roks) Nonliving things that come from Earth. José collects **rocks**. (page 154)

root (rüts) Part of a plant that holds the plant in place and takes in water for the plant. We covered the **roots** of the rose plant with soil. (page 68)

rotation (rō tā′shən) The act of turning around and around. Earth's **rotation** causes day and night. (page 322)

S

sand (sand) Tiny pieces of broken rock. We made castles of **sand** at the beach. (page 154)

screw (skrü) A simple machine used to hold things together. A **screw** was used to keep the two wooden boards together. (page 358)

season (sē′zn) One of the four parts of the year. Winter is my favorite **season**. (page 192)

seed coat (sēd kōt) The protective shell that covers and protects a seed. The **seed coat** breaks open as the plant begins to grow. (page 98)

seedling (sēd′ling) A very young plant. Rafiq planted the **seedling** in his yard. (page 98)

shadow (shad′ō) A dark shape made when something blocks light. The toy made a **shadow** on the floor. (page 286)

shelter (shel′tər) A safe place for animals and people. This wolf pup uses an old log for **shelter**. (page 12)

simple machine (sim′pəl mə shēn′) A tool with few or no moving parts that does work. The wheel and axle of this wheelbarrow is a **simple machine**. (page 356)

sleet (slēt) Sleet is frozen rain. **Sleet** made the roads very slippery. (page 189)

solid (sol′id) A kind of matter that takes up space and has its own shape. A wooden block is a **solid**. (page 218)

speed (spēd) How quickly or slowly something moves. The car moved at a very fast **speed**. (page 250)

star (stär) A big ball of hot gas. **Stars** shine brightly in the night sky. (pages 319, 324)

stem (stem) The part of a plant that carries water to the leaves. The rose's **stem** has sharp thorns. (page 68)

Sun (sun) A big ball of hot gas that makes the day sky bright. The light from the **Sun** warms the Earth. (page 319)

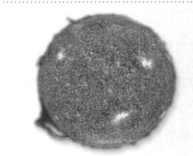

tadpole (tad′pōl′) A very young frog. Rosie caught **tadpoles** in the pond. (page 87)

technology (tek nol′ə jē) The use of scientific knowledge to solve problems. A computer is a machine that uses **technology**. (page 343)

telescope (tel′ə skōp) A tool that makes things that are far away look closer and brighter. We use a **telescope** to look at the stars in the sky. (page 324)

temperature (tem′per ə chər) How hot or cold something is. The **temperature** can be very hot in the desert. (page 184)

thermometer (thər mom′ə tər) A tool that measures temperature. We looked at the **thermometer** to see how cold it was outside. (page 184)

vibrate (vī′brāt) To move back and forth very fast. The banjo strings **vibrate** to make sounds. (page 260)

water vapor (wȯ′tər vā′pər) A form of water in the air. You cannot see **water vapor**. (page 186)

weather (weᴛʜ′ ər) What it is like outside. I like to make snowmen when the **weather** outside is cold and snowy. (page 183)

weathering (weᴛʜ′ər ing) The breaking apart and changing of rocks. **Weathering** can change the shape, size, and color of rocks. (page 158)

wedge (wej) A simple machine used to push things apart. The farmer used a shovel as a **wedge** to break up the soil. (page 356)

wetland (wet′land′) A habitat that is covered with water. Tanya saw a bullfrog when she visited the **wetland** near her home. (page 34)

wheel and axle (hwēl and ak′səl) A simple machine used to move things. A wheelbarrow has a **wheel and axle**. (page 356)

Index

This index lists the pages on which topics appear in this book. Page number after a *p* refer to a photograph or drawing.

Credits

Text

"The Frog on the Log" by Ilo Orleans from *Read-Aloud Rhymes for the Very Young* selected by Jack Prelutsky. Copyright ©1986 by Alfred A. Knopf.

"Wind" from *Some Folks Like Cats and Other Poems* by Ivy O. Eastwick. Reprinted by permission of Boyds Mills Press.

"Merry-Go-Round" from *I Like Machinery* by Dorothy Baruch.

"Taking Off" from *Very Young Verses*, edited by Barbara Peck Geismer and Antoinette Brown Suter. Copyright ©1945 by Houghton Mifflin company; Copyright ©Renewed 1972 by Barbara P. Geismer and Antoinette Brown Suter. Reprinted by permission of Houghton Mifflin Company. All Rights Reserved.

Illustrations

31–32, 34, 36, 38 Robert Hynes; 108–109 Cheryl Mendenhall; 322 Henk Dawson.

Photographs

Every effort has been made to secure permission and provide appropriate credit for photographic material. The publisher deeply regrets any omission and pledges to correct errors called to its attention in subsequent editions.

Unless otherwise acknowledged, all photographs are the property of Scott Foresman, a division of Pearson Education.

Photo locators denoted as follows: Top (T), Center (C), Bottom (B), Left (L), Right (R), Background (Bkgd).

Cover: (C) ©Tui De Roy/Minden Pictures, (Bkgd) ©Tim Davis/Corbis, (BL) Getty Images.

Front Matter: ii ©DK Images; iii (TR, B) ©DK Images; v ©DK Images; vi (B) ©DK Images, (CL) Corbis; vii Getty Images; viii (CL) Digital Vision, (BC) ©DK Images; ix (CR) ©Michael and Patricia Fogden/Corbis, (B) ©DK Images; x (TL, CL, B) ©Michael & Patricia Fogden/Corbis, (BR) ©Rick and Nora Bowers/Visuals Unlimited; xii (CL) ©Richard Price/Getty Images, (CL) ©Thomas Kitchin/Tom Stack & Associates, Inc.; xiii (CR) Stephen Oliver/©DK Images, (CR) Getty Images; xiv (CL) Getty Images, (B) ©DK Images; xv ©Frank Siteman/PhotoEdit; xvi ©Stone/Getty Images; xvii Courtesy of the London Toy and Model Museum/Paddington, London/©DK Images; xviii (CL) NASA Image Exchange, (CL) ©Roger Ressmeyer/Corbis; xix ©Lowell Georgia/Corbis; xx ©DK Images; xxii ©Douglas Faulkner/Photo Researchers, Inc.; xxiii ©William Harrigan/Lonely Planet Images; xxiv ©William Harrigan/Lonely Planet Images; xxv (BC) ©John Pontier/Animals Animals/Earth Scenes, (TR) ©Ames/NASA; xxix ©Ed Bock/Corbis; xxxi ©Little Blue Wolf Productions/Corbis; xxxii ©Andy Crawford/DK Images.

Unit A: Divider: ©Wayne R. Bilenduke/Getty Images; 1 (C) ©Sumio Harada/Minden Pictures, (TR) ©Royalty-Free/Corbis; 2 (B) Corbis, (T) ©Pat O'Hara/Corbis; 3 ©Mary Kate Denny/PhotoEdit; 5 (Bkgd) ©Pat O'Hara/Corbis, (C) ©Royalty-Free/Corbis, (TR) ©DK Images; 6 ©Pat O'Hara/Corbis; 7 (BR) ©Darrell Gulin/Corbis, (TR) ©DK Images; 8 (TR) ©Photowood, Inc./Corbis, (TL) Getty Images; 9 (TL) ©Manoj Shah/Animals Animals/Earth Scenes, (BR) ©J. & B. Photographers/Animals Animals/Earth Scenes; 10 (BL) ©Roy Morsch/Corbis, (TL) Digital Vision; 11 ©Guy Edwardes/Getty Images; 12 (BL) ©Darrell Gulin/Corbis, (C) Corbis, (TL) ©DK Images; 13 ©Dan Guravich/Corbis; 14 ©Mary Kate Denny/PhotoEdit; 16 (TL, C) ©DK Images; 17 Brand X Pictures; 20 (TL) ©Frank Lukasseck/Zefa/Corbis, (TR) ©Christine Schneider/Zefa/Corbis, (B) ©Don Mason/Corbis, (CL) ©IPS Co., Ltd./Beateworks; 21 (T,B) ©Royalty-Free/Corbis, (TC) ©DLILLC/Corbis; 22 (TC) ©Manoj Shah/Animals Animals/Earth Scenes, (B) ©J. & B. Photographers/Animals Animals/Earth Scenes; 23 (TR) ©Darrell Gulin/Corbis, (CL, C) ©DK Images; 24 (TL) Alan Schroeder/Courtesy of Sonia Ortega, (B) ©John Bova/Photo Researchers, Inc.; **Chapter 2:** 25 (C) Getty Images, (TR) ©Stephen Dalton/Photo Researchers, Inc.; 26 (C) ©W. Perry Conway/Corbis, (BL) ©Daniel J. Cox/Natural Exposures, (BR) ©David Samuel Robbins/Corbis; 27 (BR) ©Yva Momatiuk/John Eastcott/Minden Pictures, (BL) Digital Vision; 29 (Bkgd) ©W. Perry Conway/Corbis, (TR, C) ©DK Images; 30 ©W. Perry Conway/Corbis; 31 (BR) ©Taxi/Getty Images, (TR) ©Jeremy Thomas/Natural Visions; 32 (TL) ©Jeremy Thomas/Natural Visions, (BL) ©Jeffrey Lepore/Photo Researchers, Inc., (CR) ©Daniel J. Cox/Natural Exposures; 33 ©Daniel J. Cox/Natural Exposures; 34 (BC) ©Steve Maslowski/Photo Researchers, Inc., (TL) Brand X Pictures; 35 (C) ©David Samuel Robbins/Corbis, (BR) ©Joe McDonald/Corbis, (TR) ©Stone/Getty Images, (CR) Getty Images; 36 (CR) Digital Vision, (TL) ©Stone/Getty Images; 37 (CR) ©Flip Nicklin/Minden Pictures, (TR) Getty Images, (BR) ©Photographer's Choice/Getty Images; 38 (TL) ©Photographer's Choice/Getty Images, (BL) ©DK Images; 39 (BC) ©Yva Momatiuk/John Eastcott/Minden Pictures, (TC) ©Jose Fuste Raga/Corbis; 40 ©Yva Momatiuk/John Eastcott/Minden Pictures, (TR) ©Gerry Ellis/Minden Pictures; 42 (BC) ©Nigel J. Dennis/NHPA Limited, (T) ©Art Wolfe/Stone/Getty Images; 44 (TR, BR) ©Daniel J. Cox/Natural Exposures, (CL) ©David Samuel Robbins/Corbis, (CR) ©Yva Momatiuk/John Eastcott/Minden Pictures, (TR) Digital Vision; 45 (C) ©Robert Lubeck/Animals Animals/Earth Scenes, (TR) Brand X Pictures; 46 NASA; 47 (TR) Getty Images, (CL) ©Porterfield/Chickering/Photo Researchers, Inc., (BR) ©Doug Perrine/DRK Photo; 48 (BC) ©Operation Migration, Inc.; **Chapter 3:** 49 (TL) ©DK Images, (C) ©Michael Patrick O'Neill/NHPA Limited; 50 (BL) ©Richard K. LaVal/Animals Animals/Earth Scenes, (BR) ©T. Kitchin and V. Hurst/NHPA Limited, (C) Digital Vision; 51 (BR) ©Jeff Lepore/Photo Researchers, Inc., (BL) ©J.P. Ferrero/Jacana/Photo Researchers, Inc.; 53 (Bkgd) Digital Vision, (CL) Corel, (CR) ©Lynn Stone/Index Stock Imagery, (TR) ©Helen Williams/Photo Researchers, Inc.; ©54 David Fritts/Stone/Getty Images; 55 (BR) ©Steve Coombs/Photo Researchers, Inc., (TR) Getty Images; 56 (B) ©DK Images, (TL, C) ©B. Jones and M. Shimlock/NHPA Limited; 58 (TL, BL) ©Helen Williams/

Photo Researchers, Inc., (BR) ©DK Images; 59 ©Noboru Komine/Photo Researchers, Inc.; 60 (CR) ©Mitsuaki Iwago/Minden Pictures, (TR) Digital Vision, (B) ©S. Purdy Matthews/Stone/Getty Images, (TL) ©Ana Laura Gonzalez/Animals Animals/Earth Scenes; 61 ©Art Wolfe/Getty Images; 62 (BL) ©Stephen Krasemann/Stone, (CR) ©T. Kitchin and V. Hurst/NHPA Limited, (TL) ©Richard K. LaVal/Animals Animals/Earth Scenes; 63 (T) ©Richard K. LaVal/Animals Animals/Earth Scenes, (B) ©J.P. Ferrero/Jacana/Photo Researchers, Inc.; 64 (BC) ©Dante Fenolio/Photo Researchers, Inc., (TL, BC) ©DK Images; 65 (C) ©John Warden/Stone/Getty Images, (CR) ©Tom and Pat Leeson/Photo Researchers, Inc.; 66 (CR) ©DK Images, (TL) ©Jerry Young/©DK Images, (CL) ©Virginia Neefus/Animals Animals/Earth Scenes; 67 ©Chase Swift/Corbis; 70 (BR) ©Tom & Pat Leeson/Photo Researchers, Inc., (CL) Getty Images, (TL, CR) ©DK Images, (BL) ©Alan and Sandy Carey/Getty Images; 71 (CL) ©John Eastcott and Yva Momatiuk/NGS Image Collection, (BL) ©Ed Reschke/Peter Arnold, Inc., (CR, BR) ©DK Images; 72 (TL, C) ©DK Images; 73 (C, CR) ©DK Images; 74 (TR) ©H. H./Getty Images, (TC) Getty Images; 76 (Bkgd) ©Arctic National Wildlife Refuge/Getty Images, (CR) ©Art Wolfe/Getty Images, (B) ©S. Purdy Matthews/Stone/Getty Images; 77 (CR) ©Virginia Neefus/Animals Animals/Earth Scenes, (TR, BR) ©DK Images, (CR) ©Stephen Krasemann/Stone, (CC) ©Helen Williams/Photo Researchers, Inc.; 78 (CR) ©J.P. Ferrero/Jacana/Photo Researchers, Inc., (BR) ©Darrell Gulin/Corbis, (C) ©DK Images; 79 (C) Photo 24/Brand X Pictures, (CR) ©Ralph A. Clevenger/Corbis, (TR) ©DK Images; 80 (BL) ©JSC/NASA, (BR, Bkgd) NASA; **Chapter 4:** 81 ©Allen Russell/Index Stock Imagery; 82 (TL, C, BL) ©DK Images, (BR) ©Michael and Patricia Fogden/Corbis; 83 (BR) ©David Young-Wolff/PhotoEdit, (CR, BC) ©DK Images, (BL) ©George D. Lepp/Corbis; 85 (TR, C, CL) ©DK Images, (CR) Odds Farm Park/©DK Images, (Bkgd) ©Stephen Dalton/NHPA Limited; 86 ©Stephen Dalton/NHPA Limited; 87 (TR, CR, BR) ©DK Images; 88 (TL, C, B) ©DK Images; 89 ©DK Images; 90 (TR, B) ©DK Images, (TL) ©Geoff Brightling/©DK Images; 91 ©DK Images; 92 (T) ©George D. Lepp/Corbis, (B) ©Michael and Patricia Fogden/Corbis, (TL) ©DK Images; 93 (BL) George D. Lepp/Corbis, (T) ©DK Images; 94 (CR) ©T. Wiewandt/DRK Photo, (B) ©Joseph T. Collins/Photo Researchers, Inc., (TL) ©DK Images; 95 (TL) ©Jane Burton/Bruce Coleman, Inc., (C) ©Norbert Wu/Minden Pictures; 96 (BL) ©Pam Francis/Getty Images, (CR) ©Pat Doyle/Corbis; 97 (TR) ©George D. Lepp/Corbis, (B) ©Bruce Ando/Index Stock Imagery; 98 Derek Hall/©DK Images; 99 ©DK Images; 100 (TL) Matthew Ward/©DK Images, (BL) ©David Young-Wolff/PhotoEdit; 101 (BR) ©Bill Ross/Corbis, (TC) ©DK Images; 102 (B) ©DK Images, (CL) ©A. Riedmiller/Peter Arnold, Inc.; 103 ©DK Images; 104 (CL, CC, CR) Brand X Pictures, (BL, BR) ©DK Images; 105 (TR) ©Stephen Dalton/Photo Researchers, Inc., (B) ©Royalty-Free/Corbis; 106 ©Steve Terrill/Corbis; 110 (TR) ©David Young-Wolff/PhotoEdit, (TC) ©George D. Lepp/Corbis, (CL) ©Michael and Patricia Fogden/Corbis, (TL, CR) ©DK Images, (BR) ©Nicolas Granier/Peter Arnold, Inc.; 111 (TR) ©DK Images, (CL, CR) ©Jeff Foott/Bruce Coleman Collection, (C) ©Daniel W. Gotshall/Seapics; 112 ©Ed Bock/Corbis; **Chapter 5:** 113 (C) ©Jonathan Blair/Corbis, (TR) ©David Aubrey/Corbis, (BC) ©Clive Druett/Papilio/Corbis; 114 (BR) ©Gary Braasch/Corbis, (C) ©Michael & Patricia Fogden/Corbis, (T) ©Ken Lucas/Visuals Unlimited; 115 ©Hal Horwitz/Corbis; 117 (C) Getty Images, (TR, Bkgd) ©Michael & Patricia Fogden/Corbis; 118 ©Michael & Patricia Fogden/Corbis; 119 ©Michael & Patricia Fogden/Minden Pictures; 122 (B, BL) ©Michael & Patricia Fogden/Corbis, (TL) ©Michael Fogden/Animals Animals/Earth Scenes, (BR) ©Rick and Nora Bowers/Visuals Unlimited; 123 ©Kevin Schafer/NHPA Limited; 124 (TL) ©Michael & Patricia Fogden/Corbis, (BL) ©Kevin Schafer/NHPA Limited, (B) Steve Kaufman/Corbis; 125 (C) ©Rick and Nora Bowers/Visuals Unlimited, (CR) ©Kevin Schafer/NHPA Limited, (BR) ©Michael & Patricia Fogden/Corbis, (TR) ©Steve Kaufman/Corbis; 126 (B) ©Sue A. Thompson/Visuals Unlimited, (TL) ©Royalty-Free/Corbis; 127 ©David A. Northcott/Corbis; 128 (C) ©David A. Northcott/Corbis, (TC) ©Rick Poley/Visuals Unlimited, (TL) ©David A. Ponton/Mira, (TR) ©William J. Weber/Visuals Unlimited, (B) ©Sue A. Thompson/Visuals Unlimited; 129 (TC) ©Ted Levin/Animals Animals/Earth Scenes, (TL) ©Royalty-Free/Corbis, (CR) ©James Allen/Bruce Coleman, Inc.; 132 (TC) ©Michael & Patricia Fogden/Corbis, (C) ©John Shaw/Tom Stack & Associates, Inc.; 133 (TL) ©Michael & Patricia Fogden/Corbis, (CL) ©John Gerlach/Visuals Unlimited, (C) ©Tim Wright/Corbis, (C) ©William J. Weber/Visuals Unlimited, (CR) Getty Images, (CR) ©Michael Sewell/Peter Arnold, Inc., (CL) ©DK Images; 134 (TR, CL, C) ©Michael & Patricia Fogden/Corbis, (CR) ©Rick and Nora Bowers/Visuals Unlimited, (CR) ©Kevin Schafer/NHPA Limited, (TC) ©Hal Horwitz/Corbis, (BR) ©Jonathan Blair/Corbis; 135 (TR) ©David Aubrey/Corbis, (CR) Getty Images; 136 (BL) ©Kate Bennett Mendz/Animals Animals/Earth Scenes, (T, TC, C, R) Jerry Young/©DK Images, (TL, CR, CL, BR) ©DK Images; 138 (TL) ©Pat O'Hara/Corbis, (CL) ©W. Perry Conway/Corbis, (CL) ©David Fritts/Stone/Getty Images, (CL) ©Stephen Dalton/NHPA Limited, (BL) ©Michael & Patricia Fogden/Corbis; 140 ©Ian Beames/Ecoscene/Corbis; 142 ©John Watkins/Frank Lane Picture Agency/Corbis; 144 (Bkgd) ©Gerry Ellis/Minden Pictures, (TC) ©Breck P. Kent/Animals Animals/Earth Scenes, (BC) Corbis.

Unit B: Divider: ©Hiroyuki Matsumoto/Getty Images; **Chapter 6:** 145 (C) ©Steve Raymer/NGS Image Collection, (BR) ©Paul Chesley/NGS Image Collection; 146 (TL, BL) ©Barry L. Runk/Grant Heilman Photography, (BR) ©Garry D. McMichael/Photo Researchers, Inc., (CR) ©Richard Price/Getty Images, (CL) ©DK Images; 147 ©DK Images; 149 (Bkgd) ©Richard Price/Getty Images, (C) NASA; 150 ©Richard Price/Getty Images; 151 ©Thomas Kitchin/Tom Stack & Associates, Inc.; 152 (TR) Silver Burdett Ginn, (BR) ©J. Jangoux/Photo Researchers, Inc., (TL) ©Calvin Larsen/Photo Researchers, Inc., (C) ©Craig Aurness/Corbis; 153 ©Steve Dunwell/Getty Images; 154 (TL, B) ©DK Images; 155 (TL) ©Galen Rowell/Corbis, (TR) ©W. Perry Conway/Corbis, (B) ©J. Eastcott Film/NGS Image Collection; 156 (BL) ©J. P. Ferrero/Jacana/Photo Researchers, Inc., (BR) Getty Images, (C, CR) ©Barry L. Runk/Grant Heilman Photography, (TL, TC) ©DK Images; 157 ©Steve Shott/DK Images; 158 ©DK Images; 159 (TR) ©Barry L. Runk/Grant Heilman Photography, (TL) ©Michael